To The Readers of This Volume

These pages contain the personal and family history of

It is in our past that future generations will find the beginnings of who they are. This book is an attempt to give you, the reader, a peek into the life of its author and a better understanding of your family's history.

A
Private Gift
From

Table of Contents

Personal Family & History

You

What is your full name? If this is not
your given/maiden name, what was your
birth name?

Do you know how and why your name
was changed?

What is your current address?

When, where and in what town were
you born?

Is there a story about your birth that
your family would tell?

Your Father

When and where was your father born?

Why did he, or his family, come to
America? Where did they settle,
and why?

What have you been told about his
family and childhood that was
important to you?

Describe your father as a young person,
and as an adult. Who was he?

How many sisters and brothers were in
his family, what were their full names,
and when were they born?

Your Mother

When and where was your mother born?

Why did she, or her family, come to
America? Where did they settle,
and why?

What have you been told about her
family and childhood that was
important to you?

Describe your mother as a young person,
and as an adult. Who was she?

How many sisters and brothers were in
her family, what were their full names,
and when were they born?

Your Immediate Family

Were you raised by both your mother
and father? If not, with whom did you
live, and why?

Are both of your parents still living? If
so, where is their home, and how often
do you see them?

How many children were in your family?
Which one were you? What are the full
names and birthdates of your siblings?

How has your relationship with your
siblings changed over the years? Do
you feel closer to a particular brother
or sister, and, if so, why?

What did your parents teach you that
helped you succeed in life?

Your Grandparents

When and where were your mother's
parents born?

What have you been told about her
parents' lives when they were young?
When they became adults?

Is there a story your mother would tell
that illustrated what it was like to be
raised by her parents?

When and where were your father's
parents born?

What have you been told about his parents' lives when they were young? When they became adults?

Is there a story your father would tell that illustrated what it was like to be raised by his parents?

What memories do you have of your grandparents from when you were growing up?

Are any of your grandparents still alive? If so, where do they live, and how often do you see them?

Did you have a favorite grandparent, and what made your relationship special?

Coming To America

What country and town—if you know—
did each person on your family tree
(pages 26-27) come from, and when
did they come to America, if they did?

Did your family keep in touch with
anyone in the "old country?" If so,
what was their name, address and
relationship to the family?

Is there any ritual, pastime or preference
in your family today that clearly has
its roots in your family's past?

Family Life

Day To Day

What was it like growing up in your family?

Who provided the income in your family, what did they do for a living, and how well off was your family?

Was there more than one language spoken in your home, or in your parents' home? If so, what was it, and why was it kept alive or forgotten?

What did you do in the afternoons, after school, when you were growing up?

Did you have any hobbies when you were growing up? What were they, and what attracted you to them?

What did you do in the evenings, after supper, when you were growing up?

How would you spend your weekends when you were growing up?

Did you or another family member play a musical instrument? If you played an instrument, how did you learn to play?

What kind of music would your parents
listen to; what would you listen to if
you were by yourself?

What sort of magazines and books did
your family like to read? Is there a book
or group of books that were important
to you when you were growing up?

Did you have a pet? Is there a story you
or your family like to tell about it?

What was it like to go to the movies
when you were growing up, how much
did it cost, and what stars and films
were your favorites?

How and where did you spend your
summers as a child?

If your family took a vacation, where would they go, how would they get there, and what did they do?

What was it like when you went to big family gatherings as a child? Where would they be held, who would attend, and how did everyone act?

Was there a family member that you considered a "character?" What stories do you or your family tell that best illustrate that person's eccentricity?

Did anyone outside your immediate family live with you while you were growing up, such as aunts, uncles, cousins or grandparents? If so, who, for how long, and why?

Religion

What religion were your parents?

What sort of religious training or
teaching did you receive as a child?

Do you still belong to that faith? If not,
do you now adhere to another faith, and,
if so, what made you change your
religion?

If you no longer practice an organized
religion, what part does religion or
spirituality play in your life? How
and why did you come to this?

Living Places

How many places did you live while
you were growing up, where were
they, and which one do you consider
your "home town?"

What was your home town like?

Describe your house there, including its
address, size, modern conveniences, and
surroundings.

Did you have your own room? If not, with
whom did you share a room, or a bed?

What do you remember about your neighborhood and neighbors?

What would you see on a typical walk around your neighborhood that is different from what you might see today?

Notes:

School Years

Grade School & High School

Did you go to school as a child? If so, what schools did you attend for grades K-12? If you did not go to school, how were you educated?

How did you get to school each day, and what was the size of your class? If you were taught one-room style, what was the age range of your classmates?

If you attended high school, but did not graduate 12th grade, why did you drop out?

How important was formal education to your family, and how far did your parents expect your education to go? Did your family want you to pursue a specific course of study or job path?

Did you like school? What were your
favorite subjects, and why?

Did you play on any sports teams or
belong to any extracurricular clubs?

How did your opinion of yourself change
during your school years? What
influenced those changes?

Who was your best friend, and what
made that friendship endure? Are you
still close today?

During your school years, who, if anyone, did you look to for guidance and advice, and how did that person positively affect your life?

What do you remember about your high school prom?

What did you do the summer after your high school graduation?

What were your plans for the rest of your life?

College & Graduate School

If you went on to college, how old were you as a freshman, what college did you attend, and why did you pick that institution?

How much was tuition and how did you or your family pay for it?

Did you enter college already knowing what you would major in? If not, when and how did you discover your interest once you were there?

Did you graduate and, if so, in what year and with what degree? If you didn't graduate, how far did you get and why did you stop?

After college did you pursue a graduate
degree? If so, what institution did you
attend, what was your major, and how
did you pay for it?

Did you graduate, and, if so, in what year
and with what degree? If you didn't
graduate, how far did you get and why
did you stop?

After graduation from college or graduate
school, did you enter the field for which
you had studied? If not, what field did
you enter, and why?

Do you feel that you took full advantage
of what college had to offer you?

Serving Your Country

If you did not serve in the military, did you serve your country in a civilian capacity? If so, what did you do, where and when did you do it, and why did you choose to serve in that manner?

If you served in the military, did you enlist, or were you drafted? Why did you join the service? During what years did you serve, and to what branch were you attached?

Where did you receive basic training? Where were you first posted, and why? What was your serial number and initial rank?

What assignment did you like most, and how long were you posted there?

Did you see combat during your tour of
duty, and, if so, where and in what war
or military action?

Were you ever injured during combat?
What were your injuries, and where
were they first treated? Did you return
to the war?

Were you ever a prisoner of war? If so,
where were you incarcerated, and for
how long?

If you were decorated during your tour
of duty, for what were you cited?

Family Tree
Direct Lineage

Mother

You

Father

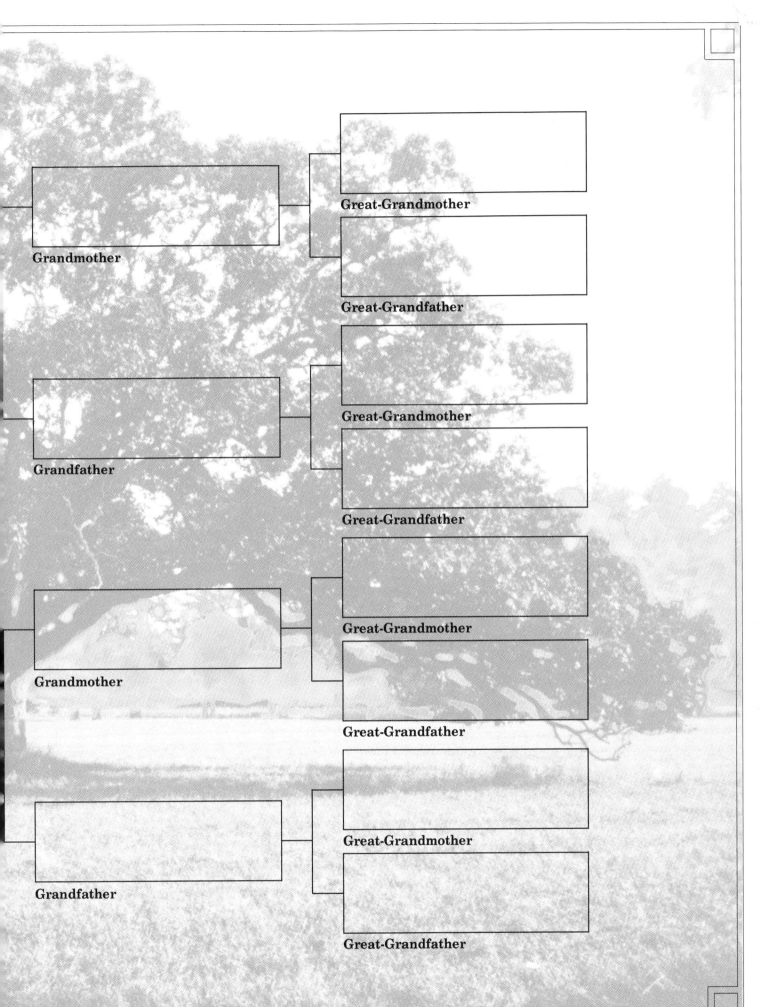

Grandmother

Grandfather

Grandmother

Grandfather

Great-Grandmother

Great-Grandfather

Great-Grandmother

Great-Grandfather

Great-Grandmother

Great-Grandfather

Great-Grandmother

Great-Grandfather

What is your most vivid memory of your service years?

If you did not make it a career, why did you decide to leave the military and what was your final rank?

Notes:

Working Your Way Through Life

Did you have any after-school or summer jobs when you were growing up? What were they, and what were your responsibilities?

Did your parents like their own jobs, and what sort of work ethic or expectations did they pass on to you?

What was your first full-time job, how old were you when you got it, how did you get it, and how long did it last?

If you have always been a homemaker, how old were you when you began keeping your own house, and what were the early years like?

How did "homemaking" change for you over the years? Have you enjoyed it?

How old were you when you left home to live on your own? Where did you live, and what did it cost?

List all the jobs you have held in your working life, with as many dates as you can remember.

Have you ever gone into business for yourself? How did your venture turn out?

When and how did you settle on a permanent career or job, if you did?

Is there another career that you wish you
had pursued instead of the path you did
choose?

If you could go back and change the way
you handled your own finances, what
would you do differently, and why?

At what age did you/do you plan to
retire? If you are already retired, do
you feel now that the arrangements you
made were adequate to sustain your
lifestyle?

How has retirement changed your life?
Were these the kinds of changes you
expected?

LOVE &ROMANCE

Teen & Adult

Do you remember your first childhood
crush? Did you ever tell that person that
you liked him/her? Did you ever date
that person?

Did you date as a teenager? If so, what
was a typical outing like? Were you
chaperoned? How late were you allowed
to stay out, and what happened if you
missed your curfew?

Who was your first real girlfriend/
boyfriend, and how did the relationship
come about?

How old were you when you gave or
received your first kiss?

Did you have a steady girlfriend/ boyfriend during your teen years? What did going steady mean, and what was considered "proper" romantic behavior?

How did you meet the people you dated as an adult?

Do you have a favorite story you like to tell about dating as a single adult?

Were you/are you happy being single? And what did you/do you want from a romantic relationship?

Courtship & Marriage

If you are married, for how long were
you single, and how many people did
you date before you met your spouse?
If you are single, why haven't you
married?

Where did you meet your spouse? What
attracted you to him/her? What did they
tell you attracted them to you?

How long did you date before you
became engaged? How and where did
you "pop" or "answer" the big question?

What did your family think of your
fiancé(e)? What did his/hers think of you?

Where did you and your fiancé(e) live
before you got married? How long was
your engagement?

On what date and where did you get
married? Where was the reception and
how many people attended?

What was your wedding like? Did you
enjoy the reception?

Is there a favorite anecdote you like to
tell about your wedding day?

Where did you spend your wedding night
and your honeymoon?

Where was the first place you lived as
a married couple, and how would you
describe the early years of your
marriage?

Are you still married? If so, how many
years have you been married? How
would you describe your marriage today?

If not, how and why did the marriage
end? Are you still friends? Did you ever
marry again? If so, when, and how has
that second (third, etc.) marriage worked
out?

Children

Becoming A Parent

Did you and your spouse discuss whether or not you wanted to have a family, and, if so, what issues came up during that discussion?

If you decided not to have children, how has it affected your relationship? How do you feel about the decision now?

If you did have children, how soon after you were married did the first baby come?

How many children did you have in all? Did all of your children survive infancy? If they survived infancy, did they reach adulthood?

Are any of your children adopted? If so, why did you choose to adopt?

What is the full name and date of birth
of each of your children?

Where do they live?

If they have finished their schooling,
where do they work, and at what job?

How often do you see your children?

Parenting

What have you enjoyed about being a
parent? What did you find most
challenging?

If you had it to do over again, what
would you change about the way
you parented your children?

What was the most difficult problem ever
brought to you by one of your children,
and how did you handle it?

How did you discipline your children?

What story do you like to tell about each
of your children that best illustrates what
they were like when they were small?

What is the best piece of advice you
ever gave your children?

What values did you strive to teach your
children when they were growing up?
What traditions did you try to pass down
to them, and, how did you accomplish
that?

What about each of your children makes
you most proud?

Did you take an active role in your children's schooling, or in community affairs? In what ways?

Did you travel as a family? Where did you go for school and summer vacations?

Did other members of your family live with you? If so, who, and did they help take care of your children?

Notes:

Leaving The Nest

If your children are grown, how did your
life change when they moved out of the
house?

Have your grown children fulfilled your
expectations for them, and what was
your reaction to the path they chose?

Are any of your children married, and, if
so, to whom are they married? When did
they get married?

Do you have any grandchildren? If so,
what is the full name and date of birth
for each of your children's children?

What do you enjoy about being a grand-parent? What do you find most challenging?

Do you have a particularly special relationship with one or more of your grandchildren, and, if so, what makes it special?

Have you become a great-grandparent? If so, what is the full name and date of birth for each child, and which of your grandchildren is the parent?

Notes:

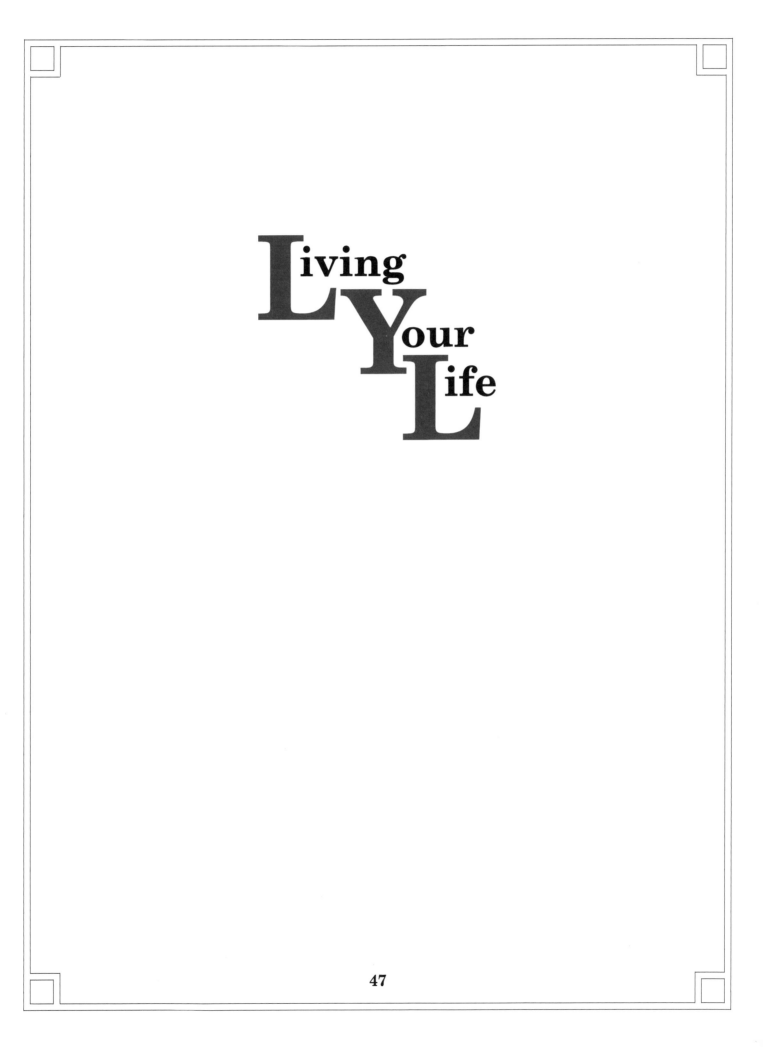

Living Your Life

Beliefs & Expectations

If you belong to a religion, has your faith
helped you during the difficult periods
of your life? If so, how?

What do you believe happens to people
after they die?

What do you think each of us owes to
the less fortunate of the world? What
have you done to help others, and, do
you feel it is/was enough?

When you judge yourself in your own mind, is there a person against whom you measure yourself? If so, who is that person and why do you look up to them?

What makes life worth living for you (In other words, why do you bother getting up in the morning?), and how has your personal answer to that question changed over the years?

What are the most important rules you've made for yourself to cope with the tragedies and adversities of life?

Life Choices

Has your life turned out the way you
thought it would when you were young?

Is there an incident or insight that
changed you and permanently altered
your future? What was it that happened,
and how did it affect you?

What is the biggest risk you ever took
in your life, and how did it work out?

How important has friendship been in
your life? How successful have you been
in making and sustaining friendships?

If you have a "best" friend, how long
have you known that person, and what
role does he or she play in your life?

If you had your life to live over again,
what, if anything, would you change?

What is the best piece of advice you were
ever given, and the best advice you ever
passed along yourself?

Looking back at your life, of what are
you most proud?

Politics & People

When did you first vote for a president, who were the candidates, and what was important to you in making your decision?

Over the years, have you belonged to one or more political parties, and, if so, what policies or positions drew you to that party?

Describe the world events that were most important in your lifetime.

A public figure once said: "If I should have to choose between my friend and my country, I hope I should have the courage to choose my friend." Do you agree or disagree with this, and why?

Who were your heroes when you were
growing up, and who are they now?

How have your heroes influenced you
over the years?

What historical events and technologies
do you feel most changed the world
during your lifetime, and what were
their effects?

Favorites Then & Now

	Then	Now			Then	Now
Holiday				Song		
Hobby				Musician		
Board Game				Symphony		
Card Game				Opera		
Outdoor Activity				Dance		
Indoor Activity				Actor		
Food				Actress		
Drink				Comedian		
Place				TV Show		
Color				Radio Program		
Animal				Spectator Sport		
Season				Participatory Sport		
Author				Athlete		
Book of Fiction				Sports Team		
Nonfiction Book				Saying		
Poem				Epithet/Cuss		
Play				Charity		
Singer				Way To Travel		

Leisure Time

How important to you is your leisure
time, and, how do you spend the
majority of it?

What do you do for exercise and how
often do you do it? What purpose does
exercise serve for you?

Do you have a pet, and, if so, what is
its name and what need does it fill in
your life?

Do you have a vacation home or a
favorite place you like to "get away" to?
And, what need does it serve?

Describe how you live today and how
close it is to your ideal of the way you
would like to live.

Predictions

What is life like today that you could
not have foreseen in your wildest
imagination when you were a child?

How do you think someone will answer
that question 100 years from now?

Are you optimistic about the future?
What do you think holds the greatest
promise for the future of the planet?
The gravest danger?

What do you expect life to be like
100 years from now?

Notes: